DOS Today

Running Vintage MS-DOS Games and Apps on a Modern Computer

by Brian Schell

ISBN: **1533614105**

ISBN-13: **978-1533614100**

DEDICATION

To all those guys who made all those games,

still going thirty-five years later

Table of Contents

INTRODUCTION

I bought my first computer in 1980, and it was one of those tiny Sinclair ZX-81 imports. I was in the tenth grade, and I played with that thing incessantly. I quickly outgrew it and moved to a Commodore VIC-20 and later a Commodore 64. I learned a lot on these early machines, including BASIC and a little machine code (they didn't really have any Assemblers for those machines and C was limited to machines way out of my budget). Still, my computing education really took off in 1986, when I got my first "PC Compatible" computer. It had a 286 processor and ran DOS 3.3 from two 5-1/4" floppy drives. It didn't have any hard drive at all.

I mastered the version of BASIC that was included with it, then picked up Turbo Pascal and got to work learning that. In the meantime, I played plenty of games, from the original SimCity to Ultima III. If I remember correctly, Ultima III was the first game of that type I ever actually took the time to beat completely. I may sound a little curmudgeonly here, but today's super high-resolution first-person shooters just don't have that kind of appeal to me.

Here we are in 2016, and I started to feel nostalgic for the days of BBSs and text-mode command lines. Today's modern computers are vastly overpowered to run old copies of MS-DOS, even if I could still find one.

Actually, even today, floppy disc-based copies of MS-DOS aren't hard to find, but most computers don't even have the hardware to install it. Does your computer even *have* a floppy drive anymore? None of mine do. I might have an old machine in the garage somewhere that I could dig out and get running again, but if I did all that, I might remember what a headache those old computers *really* were, and the nostalgia factor would dry up pretty quickly. No, I want to be able to sit here at my real desk and play those old games on my 27" Mac screen. On my modern computer, where all the hardware just works without needing "extended memory," MSCDEX CD-ROM drivers, or a special "386 Enhanced Mode." Yes, the more I think about it, the more the old DOS days had their problems. I'm not saying that modern systems like Windows 10 or OSX El Capitan are flawless, not by any stretch, but when was the last time you had to download a driver just to make your mouse work?

Still, times were simpler. There was no multitasking, so if your computer slowed down, you (usually) knew what was causing it. There was no always-on Internet connection, and getting hacked was really unlikely. *Viruses* were already a thing, but certainly not the risk they are today. Games and programs ran fast and were created to take advantage of every single clock cycle the machine allowed. Games were programmed in Assembler and machine code, not Python or Swift. Making games was *hard*, but they eked out every ounce of performance from the machines back then.

And it's not all just about the games. I write a lot. Most of the word processing and writing programs available today, such as Scrivener, Ulysses, Byword, and others offer what they call "distraction-free mode." This is a mode where the screen goes black except for your text. There aren't a bunch of little menus, windows, or popups to distract you while you work. The old PC under DOS didn't have that problem. Unless you had a special setup (TSRs or *Terminate-and-Stay-Resident applications*), your computer only ran one thing at a time. At 24x80, monitors were easy to read, and writing programs rarely had more than one font available. Don't get me wrong, this wasn't all necessarily *better*, but it was without a doubt, *simpler*.

I've heard that George R. R. Martin, the creator behind Game of Thrones, still writes all his books on an old DOS version of WordStar. He can certainly afford a modern computer, but he still uses the same tool that he became good at thirty years ago. If the old bugs have finally been squashed, why introduce new ones? Then again, maybe that's why he only releases a book every five years.

Another positive point for running old DOS software is the price. Modern games cost around $60 for the latest thing. Thirty years ago, games were commonly in the $30 to $40 range, although once in a while you could find things at a discount. Even so, adjusting for inflation, having a decent library of games and applications was about as expensive back then as it is today. If you still have the old floppies for a DOS game or app in the back of your desk drawer, your cost for those is zero. In practice, the cost for *most* of the DOS apps that you can find are nearly zero today.

The thing is, most DOS applications and games have been completely abandoned by their creators. *Some* of these old games have been officially released into the public domain by their creators and are now available for free. On the other hand, *most* of these old programs are simply what has become known as "abandonware." Their creators have moved on to other projects, new careers, or since it has been thirty years, some have even died in the meantime. The legal aspect of getting these apps is a little shaky; they are technically still under copyright, but the fact is that the creators probably don't really care anymore. Even in the case of games that still exist, the legal position is unclear. If you play the 1985 version of SimCity, does that really detract from the game's creators today? I would argue that it does not; if you like playing the old version in an emulator, you're very likely to go out and try the 2016 edition. Regardless of the gray legal position of abandonware, we'll talk about how and where to get your games in a later chapter.

Note on terminology: Throughout the book, I will use the terms "App," "Application," and "Program" interchangeably. The term "App" used as it is today didn't exist in the days of DOS, but younger readers may be unfamiliar with calling a game a "program" or "application." The term "App" isn't strictly correct, but it's the common term today.

Brian Schell

WHAT IS DOS?

Every computer ever made has *some* form of DOS, or Disk Operating System; it's how the CPU part of the computer knows how to operate the various disk drives and deal with input and output. More specifically, MS-DOS is short for "Microsoft Disk Operating System," which has been further shortened to a more generic "DOS" label. It's an operating system for x86-based personal computers that was mostly developed by Microsoft. It was the most commonly used member of the DOS family of operating systems, and was the main operating system for IBM PC compatible personal computers during the 1980s to the mid-1990s, when it was gradually superseded by operating systems offering a graphical user interface (GUI), in various generations of the graphical Microsoft Windows operating system by Microsoft Corporation. Development on MS-DOS ended around the year

2000, as it had been all but replaced by Windows 95/98 and Windows NT/2000 operating systems by that time. [1]

Still, it's been twenty or thirty years since the heyday of DOS. Why would you want to use it now? There's Windows 10, and OS X El Capitan, and Linux in a hundred flavors (all for free!) not to mention mobile operating systems like iOS and Android. Why would anyone want to bother with DOS?

The main reason is *because* it's limited. There was no networking built in with DOS, so it was actually a pretty secure system. There was no Internet in those days, at least for most people, so there are no hidden back doors or security flaws.

There was no *real* multitasking, and the hardware choices and options were far more limited then. This simplicity makes it very useful for Implementing embedded systems and single-purpose machines. There aren't a hundred threaded background processes running beneath your chosen application, there is just the main program and the operating system itself.

And then there's the games...

There were many thousands of games created for DOS. Some of them, like SimCity, Quake, Oregon Trail, and Tomb Raider, are still recognizable

---

[1]   From Wikipedia- https://en.wikipedia.org/wiki/MS-DOS

"brands" that have evolved and are available today in updated versions. Others, like the Ultima series, Wing Commander series, and thousands of others, have not been updated and are essentially obsolete, unable to run on modern computers without some trickery. These games were loads of fun decades ago, and they still are... *if you know how to make them work!*

Non-Gaming / Productivity

The largest demand for old DOS software is without a doubt in the area of video games. There were tens of thousands of games, and anyone who played any back then had their favorites. Nostalgia is a powerful motivator sometimes! Some of the games were the purest examples of garbage, while others deservedly gained their place in history as "eternal classics."

Still, believe it or not, people used computers for non-gaming purposes too. Back before Microsoft introduced Word and Excel, the two biggest business-related applications were WordPerfect 5.1 and Lotus 1-2-3. Before Access came along, dBase III and dBase IV ruled the roost in databases. Most other applications that we use today had some kind of previous incarnation in the DOS world.

One interesting application that existed for DOS that never really made the transition over to Windows were BBS, or bulletin board systems. These were computers set up by hobbyists that others would call into directly with telephones connected through modems. They offered multi-player games and files to download, as well as messaging similar to today's email. Systems like WildCat and TBBS were great fun for hobbyists, but they never found a practical niche after the Internet exploded. There *are*, however, still some bulletin board systems that you can still dial into just like the old days, but more common are BBSs that can be reached through Telnet via the Internet. Those are beyond the scope of this book, but keep in mind that these are one area where DOS actually surpassed the newer operating systems in variety and power.

Installation Challenges

There are two basic ways to deal with getting DOS up and running on a modern computer. The simplest, and the original, method is that you can set aside a hard drive partition and install the operating system just as you would have thirty years ago. This is the way Microsoft meant for DOS to be installed, so it seems like this would be the ideal solution. Unfortunately, there are a couple of complications to this:

1. Most computers today don't have floppy disk drives, and DOS didn't (originally) come on a CD-ROM. Even so, many modern systems don't even include a CD-ROM drive anymore. Still, this need not be a problem, as external floppy and CD-ROM drives can still be bought through sites such as Amazon or eBay, as well as many others.

2. Even when you do finally get your software installed, it may run way too fast on current machines. Although productivity applications like WordPerfect would probably still work well, many, if not most, games are essentially unplayable, even if they work at all.

3. Since you most likely aren't going to install it on a machine all by itself, you need to come up with some way of partitioning your hard drive so that you can run both DOS and Windows 10 (or whatever). Also, if you *were* planning on putting it on a machine all by itself, there are serious limitations to how big a hard drive partition you could use with DOS.

4. MS-DOS as it was originally created only works on PCs. If you have a Mac system, you are out of luck.

5. MS-DOS doesn't natively support CD-ROMs, Sound or Audio, USB devices (not even a mouse), or most other recent hardware, so chances are really good that you will run into some kind of hardware compatibility issue. Most modern devices don't include any kind of DOS driver software, and in most cases, none have even been created.

These sound like pretty insurmountable problems, and the list just gets worse the further down you go. Fortunately, there is a solution:

Emulation

Emulation is the imitation of behavior of a computer or other electronic system with the help of another type of computer/system. Simply put, we can make your PC, Mac, or Linux computer *think* it's running DOS in what is called a "virtual machine."

There are two methods of doing this that we will introduce in this book, but there are other alternatives available. The first is DOSBox, an app that "pretends" to be a computer running MS-DOS. You install the app, and you're basically done. You run the program from within OSX or Windows, and you'll get a little window with a DOS prompt that allows you to do whatever you want, all inside a window inside your regular computer's operating system.

There are serious benefits to doing this:

1. You can install from image files downloaded from the Internet. You don't need to physically access floppy disks.

2. The speed of the emulation is adjustable. You can make your virtual machine either faster or slower as the need arises.

3. You don't need to partition your hard drive. Everything runs *within* the emulator. All you have to install is the basic software.

4. Emulators work on most any system. You can emulate DOS on a PC, a Mac, a Linux Machine, even a Raspberry Pi.

5. Since the whole shebang is just another application running in your modern operating system, it has access to your mouse, sound hardware, printer, and most other hardware that already works on your computer.

The only real *disadvantage* of emulation is that making one machine "pretend" to be another requires a good amount of computing horsepower. This is one reason that running Mac software on a PC and vice-versa isn't common. It *can* be done, but emulating a complex machine like a current Mac Or Windows 10 PC takes a lot of processor power, and emulators for these modern machines tend to run slowly and have problems.

The thing is, MS-DOS was designed for computers that ran vastly slower than today's machines. Today's machines can easily emulate a DOS computer and have plenty of processor horsepower left over.

Although we'll briefly touch on installing DOS the original way, most of this book is going to focus on emulation. It works, it works well, and it's relatively easy.

DOSBOX

You can find DOSBOX at *http://www.dosbox.com*, and it works on Windows, Mac OSX, and Linux operating systems. This is not a full-scale operating system. It's an emulator program, which means it runs in a window (or full-screen if you want) within OSX or Windows 10. You don't need to mess with partitions, or risk ruining your computer; it's just another app that "pretends" to be a DOS command line.

My screen shots below are from OSX El Capitan, the latest version of the Mac operating system as of early 2016. If you are running Windows, the screens look mostly the same.

Go to Dosbox.com and download the current version of the app. The version as of this writing is 0.74. This has been current since September 2012, so keep in mind the software doesn't change much anymore. This shouldn't really be a concern; it's a fully-working version of a "locked-up" program (they aren't making changes to the original MS-DOS any more either), there's not really a need for a lot of updates. Anyway, download the file.

On OSX, it comes through as a .DMG file, and in Windows, you'll have a .ZIP file:

Open it, and you'll see something like this:

All you need to do to run it is just double-click, like any other app icon. You'll see something like this:

```
▓ ▓ ▓    DOSBox 0.74. Cpu speed:   3000 cycles, Frameskip 0, Program:  DOSBOX
Welcome to DOSBox v0.74

For a short introduction for new users type: INTRO
For supported shell commands type: HELP

To adjust the emulated CPU speed, use ctrl-F11 and ctrl-F12.
To activate the keymapper ctrl-F1.
For more information read the README file in the DOSBox directory.

HAVE FUN!
The DOSBox Team http://www.dosbox.com

Z:\>SET BLASTER=A220 I7 D1 H5 T6

Z:\>
```

And you'll be greeted with a hopefully friendly-looking Z:> prompt. If you're familiar with or remember the old DOS, it didn't look quite like this. The blue box at the top gives some special instructions about how to get help, and the prompt is a Z: instead of the C: (or A:) that you might remember. That's OK.

Just to reassure yourself that it actually works, try the simplest of DOS commands. At the prompt, type DIR and hit the enter/return key:

```
▓ ▓ ▓    DOSBox 0.74. Cpu speed:   3000 cycles, Frameskip 0, Program:  DOSBOX
Z:\>dir
Directory of Z:\.
COMMAND   COM              20 01-10-2002 12:34
AUTOEXEC  BAT              32 01-10-2002 12:34
KEYB      COM              20 01-10-2002 12:34
IMGMOUNT  COM              20 01-10-2002 12:34
BOOT      COM              20 01-10-2002 12:34
INTRO     COM              20 01-10-2002 12:34
RESCAN    COM              20 01-10-2002 12:34
LOADFIX   COM              20 01-10-2002 12:34
MEM       COM              20 01-10-2002 12:34
MOUNT     COM              20 01-10-2002 12:34
MIXER     COM              20 01-10-2002 12:34
CONFIG    COM              20 01-10-2002 12:34
     12 File(s)           252 Bytes.
      0 Dir(s)              0 Bytes free.

Z:\>
```

If you go back to the old days, you'll remember some of these. COMMAND.COM was the main "kernel" of the operating system, and AUTOEXEC.BAT was the file you could customize to automatically start your programs.

There are some new things here. The old DOS didn't have INTRO.COM, MOUNT.COM, or a couple of the others. These have been added to make the system work on a modern computer.

Originally, DOS was meant to load from a single floppy disk and when ready to use would show an A: prompt. Later on, after hard drives had been made practical for home use (yes, I really said that), they went to a C: prompt. The window in front of you defaults to a Z: prompt.

You'll need to tell DOSBOX where your games and apps are stored. To show you how this all works, I'm going to skip ahead a little bit and assume you have a game downloaded. The game I'm using for an example is called JOUST. On my Mac, my game is in the "Downloads" folder. At the Z: prompt, type in the following:

mount d

```
Z:\>dir
Directory of Z:\.
COMMAND  COM              20 01-10-2002 12:34
AUTOEXEC BAT              32 01-10-2002 12:34
KEYB     COM              20 01-10-2002 12:34
IMGMOUNT COM              20 01-10-2002 12:34
BOOT     COM              20 01-10-2002 12:34
INTRO    COM              20 01-10-2002 12:34
RESCAN   COM              20 01-10-2002 12:34
LOADFIX  COM              20 01-10-2002 12:34
MEM      COM              20 01-10-2002 12:34
MOUNT    COM              20 01-10-2002 12:34
MIXER    COM              20 01-10-2002 12:34
CONFIG   COM              20 01-10-2002 12:34
    12 File(s)           252 Bytes.
     0 Dir(s)              0 Bytes free.

Z:\>mount d ~/Downloads
Drive D is mounted as local directory /Users/brianschell/Downloads/

Z:\>_
```

and it will respond as above, "Drive D is mounted
as local directory /Users/brianschell/Downloads/"
Notice that this is the FULL OSX pathname. I could
have used the longer pathname

mount d /Users/brianschell/Downloads

Which would have worked just as well. On
Windows or Linux, you'll type a very similar
command line.

What this does is create a virtual disk drive called
D: and displays the files which are actually stored in
the long pathname on your "real" computer. More
specifically with my example, it made a D: drive
and put everything in my Downloads directory into
it.

I could do another DIR command to see what I
have. The next step is to go wherever the game or
app that you want to load is. To do this, you use the
CD (Change Directory) command. My Joust game
is in a directory called JOUST, so I type

D: (to change to the new "D" drive)

CD JOUST (to move to where the game is located)

I can do another DIR and see the following:

```
D:\JOUST>dir
Directory of D:\JOUST\.
.              <DIR>          13-02-2016  6:45
..             <DIR>          13-02-2016  6:45
JOUST    DOC         5,982 19-04-1990 21:35
JOUST    EXE        47,052 17-04-1990 23:47
JOUST    HIS           110 13-02-2016  6:47
     3 File(s)        53,144 Bytes.
     2 Dir(s)    262,111,744 Bytes free.

D:\JOUST>W_
```

Yup. The JOUST.EXE is the main game file. Depending on what you want to load, there could be dozens of files here, but this game only has three. The JOUST.DOC is a Microsoft Word document with some information about the game. JOUST.HIS is a file created by the game to hold temporary data, probably saving a persistent "high score" table or something.

To run the game, just type the name of the file without the EXE extension. Just type

JOUST

And the game will begin:

Press a key on the keyboard as the game instructs, and after a little configuration, the game begins. This simple game has three keys used to play: Z and X moves my bird right and left, and my Option key makes him fly. It's always important to look for instructions, as the controls on old games aren't always intuitive.

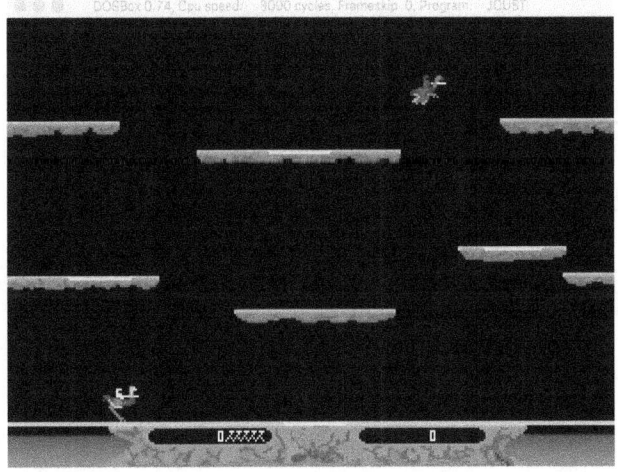

And Boom! I have a working game from 1990. I can play and kill all the jousting ostriches until I get bored with that. Even the sound works! When I am finished playing, I hit the "ESC" key or "Q" or whatever it takes to exit the game.

Once I'm back at the DOS prompt, I can type

CD .. To move up a level in the directory structure

Or CD / To move to the top level of the "hard drive"

Actually CD \ works too, which is something you couldn't do with the original DOS. If I want to change to another game I already have downloaded, say the chess game called "Nero 5," I can CD into that directory with

CD NERO5

And type the command to start that game:

NERO5

Which brings it right up:

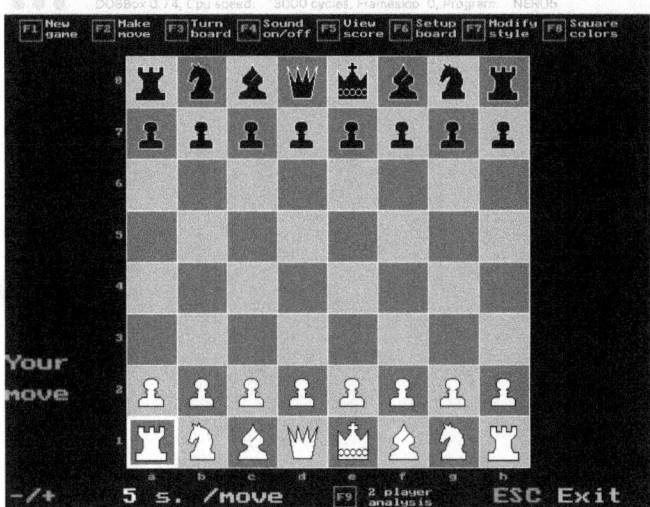

So there we have it. A quick and easy install along with how to get things running. For many games and apps, this may be all you need to know.

VIRTUALBOX

You can find VirtualBox available for free at *http://www.virtualbox.org* and it works on Windows, Mac OSX, and Linux operating systems. This is not a full-scale operating system. It's another emulator program, which means it runs in a window (or full-screen if you want) within OSX, Windows, or whatever.

The primary difference between VirtualBox and DOSBox is that DOSBox is custom-designed to run DOS and nothing else. It's dead-simple to install, but it's *only* for DOS. With VirtualBox, you can install any version of DOS, or any other operating system within the emulator. You can run DOS, Linux, old versions of Windows XP or Vista, Solaris, or most anything else. You can even run multiple operating systems side-by-side. I use it to run MS-DOS 6.22 and Ubuntu Linux on my Mac, sometimes simultaneously. I get the best of all three worlds!

If DOSBox has worked for you, and it does everything you want in DOS, then you can probably skip VirtualBox, as it's overkill for many people. Still, if the ability to experiment with other operating systems on the fly sounds appealing, or if there's some incompatibility where DOSBox won't run your specific application, then proceed with the VirtualBox installation.

Once again, the screen shots below are from OSX El Capitan, the latest version of the Mac operating system as of early 2016. If you are running Windows, the screens will look mostly the same.

Go to VirtualBox.org and download the current version of the app. The version as of this writing is 5.0.14. Unlike DOSBox, the VirtualBox system is updated regularly and often, so there's probably something newer than that available by the time you read this. On OSX, it comes through as a .DMG file, and in Windows, you'll have a .ZIP file:

Double-click on it, and the installer (For OS X) will look like this:

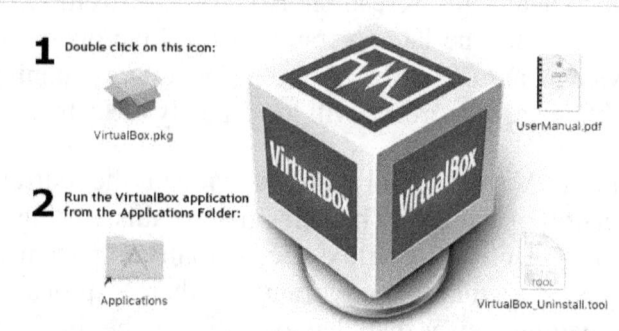

Just do what it says: Click and drag the brown VirtualBox.pkg to the Applications folder. The you can navigate to your Applications folder and click on the VirtualBox icon.

As I said, this system allows you to install any operating system within a VirtualBox. That said, you actually have to obtain a copy of that operating system—it doesn't come with DOS, or anything else for that matter.

The following instructions use the files below:

Name	^	Date Modified	Size	Kind
▼ 📁 msdos622		Feb 15, 2016, 6:20 PM	--	Folder
boot.img		Feb 15, 2016, 6:25 PM	1.5 MB	NDIF Disk Image
cd-driver.img		Feb 15, 2016, 6:25 PM	1.5 MB	NDIF Disk Image
Disk 1.img		Feb 15, 2016, 6:26 PM	1.5 MB	NDIF Disk Image
Disk 2.img		Feb 15, 2016, 6:26 PM	1.5 MB	NDIF Disk Image
Disk 3.img		Feb 15, 2016, 6:26 PM	1.5 MB	NDIF Disk Image
Disk 4.img		Feb 15, 2016, 6:27 PM	1.5 MB	NDIF Disk Image
docs.img		Feb 15, 2016, 6:26 PM	1.5 MB	NDIF Disk Image
msdos622-win311.nfo		Feb 15, 2016, 6:22 PM	548 bytes	Document
vbox-install-tuto.txt		Feb 15, 2016, 6:22 PM	5 KB	Plain Text Document
▼ 📁 win311		Feb 15, 2016, 6:16 PM	--	Folder
apps.iso		Feb 15, 2016, 6:27 PM	139 MB	ISO Disk Image
▶ 📁 disk-images		Feb 15, 2016, 6:20 PM	--	Folder
win311.iso		Feb 15, 2016, 6:26 PM	13.3 MB	ISO Disk Image

If you have an actual floppy disk drive in your computer, then insert your DOS disk #1 into the drive and point VirtualBox to whatever pathname your system uses to access that drive for the following steps.

I don't have a floppy drive attached to my system, so I downloaded these files through BitTorrent. Note that this probably isn't legal unless you own legitimate installation diskettes. I really do have a legal copy of MS-DOS sitting in my desk drawer, so I don't have any ethical quandaries about doing this. The files above are found easily online, and I have explained how to get them in the chapter "Where to Get Games and Software."

After the main VirtualBox application has started, then it's time to get it set up. The main screen looks something like this.

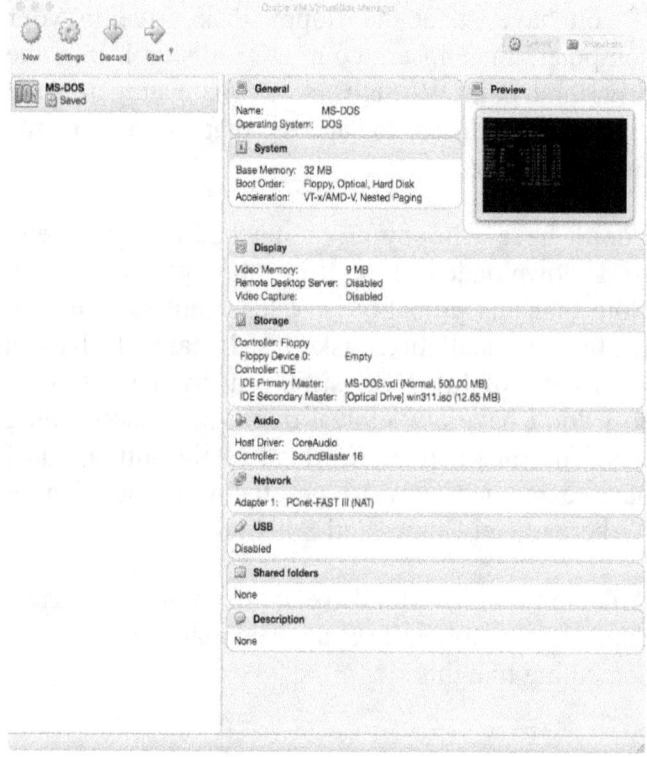

1. Choose "New" and create a virtual machine (VM) with 32MB RAM and a 500gb hard disk. This is going to be bigger and better equipped than any actual computer from the DOS era.

2. In "Settings" change:

- "System" > "Acceleration"

    - Uncheck "Enable vt-x/amd-v"

- "Storage"

- Click "floppy+" > "choose disk" and get "msdos622" > "disk 1.img" (Or wherever you have Disk 1 of MS-DOS Stored)

- "Network" > "Advanced"

  - Select "PCnet-PCI II (am79c970a)"add floppy controller".

Now, click "Start" To boot the new virtual machine and follow the DOS 6.22 setup instructions from this point forward.

If formatting hangs, then reboot the VM (press CTRL to escape the VM screen, then "Machine" > "Reset" in the VirtualBox menu). Press the F8 key at bootup to get a DOS prompt. Answer "Y" to the first question and "N" to the second. At the DOS prompt ("a:") type "format c:" enter and follow the procedure. Keep in mind that all the commands you type will only affect the VIRTUAL disk and VIRTUAL computer, not the real computer. You can not hurt anything on your real computer while inside the virtual machine.

Reboot when it asks for it. Continue with the DOS setup, changing the floppies when it asks ("devices" > "floppy devices" > "choose a virtual floppy disk file").

1. When setup has finished, reboot the virtual machine to get a DOS prompt.

The following steps are optional, but necessary if you want DOS to be able to access software on a CD-ROM (Or software that looks for a CD-ROM when installing— Even if you are downloading games).

1. Change the floppy to "cd-driver.img".

2. At the DOS prompt, type :

   copy a:c*. **c:**
   then hit the enter key (confirm overwrite with "y")

   copy a:d*. **c:dos**
   then hit enter.

3. Reboot.

And you're good to go. Click the green arrow for "Start" and watch your system boot up.

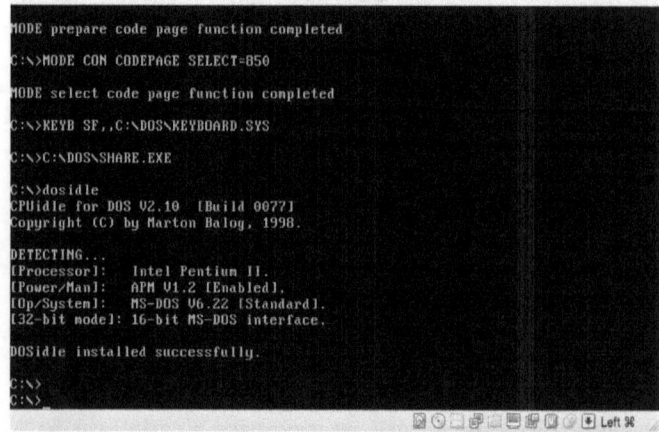

OTHER POSSIBILITIES

DOSEMU

DOSEMU, yet another emulator much like DOSBox, can be found at *http://sourceforge.net/projects/dosemu*. This one specifically runs under Linux.

FreeDOS

If you can't find get ahold of a legal copy of MS-DOS or you want to try something a little different, FreeDos may be for you. FreeDOS is a complete, free, DOS-compatible operating system that you can use to play classic DOS games, run legacy business software, or develop embedded systems.

Any program that works on MS-DOS *should* also run on FreeDOS.

It doesn't cost anything to download and run FreeDOS. Even better, you can view and edit the source code. All FreeDOS programs are distributed under the GNU General Public License or a similar open source software license.

FREEDOS can be found at *http://www.freedos.org/*

FREEDOS works quite well under VirtualBox, or, if you happen to have an actual, vintage 80s or 90s-era machine handy, it can be installed on that and replace the old operating system on that. If you cannot lay your hands on an actual copy of MS-DOS, don't want to mess with "pirate sites," or are simply a lover of open source software, you'll definitely want to look into this option.

In the screenshot above, I am running FREEDOS inside of VirtualBox, which works just fine. Another option, assuming you have an old enough computer, is to actually install FREEDOS as a "real" active operating system.

Brian Schell

WHERE TO GET GAMES AND SOFTWARE

Used Game Shops

You won't find any DOS software at your local big box store, or even on the majority of web shopping places anymore. There are a handful of used game stores that may have old software, but since the floppies those games are stored on are a bit unreliable at this age, even many used game stores have stopped carrying games on floppies. Still, it's worth a look if you have a local vintage computer shop.

EBay

If you have some specific commercial software in mind, one option here is to look for it on eBay. There's even a chance you can find a still-sealed copy of whatever you're looking for that may have sat in a warehouse for decades. You just never know until you look. For non-gaming applications that may have never been super-popular, this is probably the best way to go.

Gog.com

This is a unique site. They sell a lot of recent games, but they specialize in downloadable versions of older games. These aren't free, but they are relatively inexpensive, with most games being priced between $5 and $10. They often have sales. At the time of this writing, for example, they have Wing Commander III (the one with Mark Hamill and Malcolm McDowell) for $2.39. They don't have too many really obscure titles, but if you're looking for games that were big "back in the day," they may have it. Plus, they have support forums if you need help getting things going.

BitTorrent and "Pirate" Sites

BitTorrent isn't a specific site or program, it's a method of transferring files. You'll need a client app to download software. *uTorrent* and *Transmission* are excellent systems that work on various platforms.

Once you have the client app of your choice, you search a Torrent site for whatever it is that you want. One of the largest and most well-known of these sites is *http://ThePirateBay.se*. You can find just about anything you ever wanted there, whether it be old software, new software, music, movies, or most anything else.

As the name of the site says, it's a *pirate* site, which makes a lot, if not most of what you find there legally on the shady side. Still, if you own the floppies for a game and want to simply download a file that you can use without installing a floppy drive, you're probably OK doing that. Also, be aware that if you try downloading software that runs natively on your computer (as opposed to running in an emulator like DOSBox), then viruses are a potential risk. Use sites like these at your own risk.

Simply doing a search for a specific old DOS game probably won't turn up much. DOS games are a niche nowadays, and collectors have batched together hundreds, or even thousands of games into collections that you can download all at once.

As you can see in the screenshot, the first listing includes 749 games in one collection. The second says it has "Almost 3000 Games for DOS/PC" and some of the others will have even more. It's very likely that you can find any game you remember in one of these collections.

It's not just for games. Here's a search I did for "DOS 6.22"

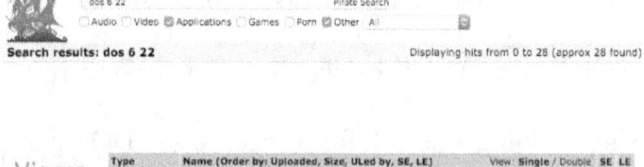

The first one in the list even specifically says it works with Virtualbox.

I was able to quickly search for "WordPerfect 5.1" and find a working copy of that, so remember this isn't just for games.

Again, working with software from these sites is risky, but they are one possible source to pick up a huge number of games. I'm very much against the idea of piracy, and I'm certainly not advocating stealing anything. If the truth is told though, most of the manufacturers of these games are long since defunct, and in all practical ways, no one cares anymore.

Abandonware

According to Wikipedia, abandonware is a product, typically software, ignored by its owner and manufacturer, and for which no product support is available. Although such software is usually still under copyright, the owner may not be tracking or enforcing copyright violations. Abandonware is one case of the general concept of *orphan works*.[2]

And that pretty well explains it. A huge amount of old software is technically still owned by some company, but the company may not care what you do with it at this point in time. Other titles had their parent companies dissolve, or were merged into other companies so many times that their back catalog of games has been largely forgotten.

Many of the games out there fall under this category. Someone, somewhere still owns the copyright to every software title ever written, but that doesn't mean that the owners intend to do anything about it.

Most of the game found on "pirate" sites like ThePirateBay, mentioned in the previous section,

---

[2] *Wikipedia - https://en.wikipedia.org/wiki/Abandonware*

fall under this category. They are technically pirated games, but there's a very good chance that no one cares anymore.

Other games and software are owned by programmers and companies that realize that time has passed them by, and they have generously, and officially, released their works into the public domain. These are completely free to download and even modify if you have the ability and knowledge.

Here are three sites you can find and load games that are generally less "gray" than downloading them from a pirate site.

http://Archive.org

http://www.dosgamesarchive.com

http://www.abandonia.com

ADDITIONAL TIPS AND TRICKS

So we've gotten the basic DOS system installed, one way or another, but there are a lot of things that the default system cannot do.

Speed Adjustment

One of the most common problems with DOSBox is that it runs games too fast. Considering that the computer sitting in front of you is quite literally thousands of times faster than machines from the 1980's, that probably shouldn't come as a surprise. Even considering that your computer is running DOS on top of Windows or OSX, there's still plenty of leftover CPU power.

To slow down the DOS system, press CTRL-F11, repeatedly if necessary. To speed things up, use CTRL-F12

Automount

Once you've run DOSBox a few times, remembering to type "mount c ~/Pathname" will start getting old pretty quickly. Fortunately, you don't need to do this. There is a file that contains commands that are executed every time you start the DOSBox app:

(Windows) "Start/WinLogo Menu"->"All Programs"->DOSBox-0.74->Options

(Linux) ~/.dosbox/dosbox-0.74.conf

(MAC OS X) "~/Library/Preferences/DOSBox 0.74 Preferences"

So, for example, if I want to automate the mounting of a directory as my new DOS C: drive, I open one of the three files above and add:

mount c "~/Desktop/DOS Games"

or something similar depending on where your games and apps are stored. That's it. Save the file and restart your DOSBOX. In my own file, I've added the line above, as well as the DOS commands CLS (Clear Screen) and DIR (show current directory).

mount c "~/Desktop/DOS Games"

c:

CLS

DIR

… and when I start DOSBox, I see this:

Adding joysticks and other hardware

If you're an old-timer who remembers the "joys" of making a joystick work under the original DOS, you can rejoice. Things have not only gotten a lot easier, but they have gotten more reliable as well.

There are two main steps involved with getting a joystick to work. First, you need to make the real computer "see" the joystick, and the second is to make the game or virtual computer you want to play actually use the joystick.

If you are a Windows user, you can probably stop reading right here. Just plug in your modern, USB-compatible joystick and it'll probably work just fine with Windows. With Mac, joysticks may not be quite as easy. There are apps available such as Joystick Mapper *http://joystickmapper.com* that will allow you to plug in most kinds of USB joysticks into your Mac. It works well with X-Box and PS/4 controllers, and those are a couple of the most easily-accessible sticks out there.

BASIC DOS COMMANDS

DOS commands are entered through a very plain-looking (by today's standards) all-text command line.

```
CD0:  IDE0 Secondary-master, VBOX CD-ROM, ATA-33.

Modules using memory below 1 MB:

  Name        Total              Conventional         Upper Memory
  --------  ----------------   ----------------     ----------------
  SYSTEM    172,432  (168K)     10,464   (10K)      161,968  (158K)
  HIMEMX      2,128   (2K)       2,128    (2K)            0    (0K)
  COMMAND     4,064   (4K)       3,024    (3K)        1,040    (1K)
  DOSLFN     12,464  (12K)      12,464   (12K)            0    (0K)
  UIDE          960   (1K)         960    (1K)            0    (0K)
  SHSUCDX    11,152  (11K)           0    (0K)       11,152   (11K)
  FDAPM         928   (1K)           0    (0K)          928    (1K)
  SHARE       9,312   (9K)           0    (0K)        9,312    (9K)
  MOUSE       3,104   (3K)           0    (0K)        3,104    (3K)
  Free      633,936 (619K)     624,976  (610K)        8,960    (9K)
Drives Assigned
Drive  Driver   Unit
D:  FDCD0001    0
2 drive(s) available.
Done processing startup files C:\FDCONFIG.SYS and C:\AUTOEXEC.BAT
Type HELP to get support on commands and navigation

Welcome to the FreeDOS 1.1 operating system (http://www.freedos.org)
C:\>_
```

The "C:>" prompt on the bottom line of the screenshot indicates that we are currently working on the "C" drive, which was typically the boot-up hard drive. Other common drive letters were the "A" drive, used for the floppy drive, and "D" which was most commonly used for a CD-ROM drive. There were other possibilities, such as systems with two floppies that would have both an "A" and a "B" floppy. Systems with more than one hard drive or multiple hard drive partitions could have drive letters that came after "C." It was pretty flexible.

To change to working on another drive, you type

    D:

and press the Enter key to change to the "D" drive.

    A: <enter>

…Would switch you over to the first floppy drive, and so on.

Once you were on the drive that you wanted, you could move through directories (what are now usually called "folders" in most systems) by typing

    CD "DOS"

at the prompt. CD stands for "change directory" and would change your working directory to the "DOS" directory. Note that DOS has a maximum filename length of eight characters and (sometimes) a three-letter file extension, COMMAND.COM and AUTOEXEC.BAT were common examples.

If you are inside a directory, you could move up a directory level by typing

CD ..

to move up a level, or

CD \

To move all the way up to the root directory.

Of course, you may want to *see* what files are in the directory, so the

DIR

command will list all files in the current directory.

```
Z:\>dir
Directory of Z:\.
COMMAND  COM              20 01-10-2002 12:34
AUTOEXEC BAT              32 01-10-2002 12:34
KEYB     COM              20 01-10-2002 12:34
IMGMOUNT COM              20 01-10-2002 12:34
BOOT     COM              20 01-10-2002 12:34
INTRO    COM              20 01-10-2002 12:34
RESCAN   COM              20 01-10-2002 12:34
LOADFIX  COM              20 01-10-2002 12:34
MEM      COM              20 01-10-2002 12:34
MOUNT    COM              20 01-10-2002 12:34
MIXER    COM              20 01-10-2002 12:34
CONFIG   COM              20 01-10-2002 12:34
      12 File(s)         252 Bytes.
       0 Dir(s)            0 Bytes free.

Z:\>
```

To run a program, you simply type the filename, omitting the .EXE or .COM extension. Note that in DOS the only files that can be run end with

.EXE

.COM

.BAT

Other files are just for data. Again, you don't need to type the extension to make the program run.

So in the example in the screenshot above, all those files are executable. If you wanted to run the MEM.COM program, you would simply type

    mem

(or "MEM" since it's not case-sensitive) and hit the Enter key.

You should see output something like this:

```
C:\>mem

     632 Kb free conventional memory
      63 Kb free upper memory in 1 blocks (largest UMB 63 Kb)
   15168 Kb free extended memory
   15168 Kb free expanded memory

C:\>
```

If you are familiar with UNIX or LINUX, these commands should look somewhat familiar. On the other hand, if you are only used to modern versions of Windows or are coming from a Mac background, this may be a whole new world for you. All operating systems, Windows and Mac included, still have a command line, but as the years pass, they are needed less and less. Some users have never needed to use one, but they *are* still there, and learning to use it opens up a whole new level of technical competence.

Navigating around drives and directories, getting directory listings, and running programs is really all you *need* to know to run old games and application software. If you want to learn more DOS commands, I would recommend the classic "DOS for Dummies" book. It's available on Amazon and there are used copies available for as little as a penny (plus shipping). It's a fun trivia fact that

"DOS for Dummies" just happened to be the *first* book in the insanely-popular "For Dummies" series.

ABOUT THE AUTHOR

Brian Schell is a College IT Instructor who has an extensive background in computers dating back to the 1980s.

Currently, he writes on a wide array of topics from computers, to world religions, to ham radio, and even releases the occasional short horror tale.

He'd love to hear your stories of success and failure with DOS games. If there's something you would like to see in a future edition of the book, drop him a note.

Contact him at:

Twitter: @BrianSchell
Facebook: http://www.Facebook.com/Brian.Schell
Web: http://BrianSchell.com